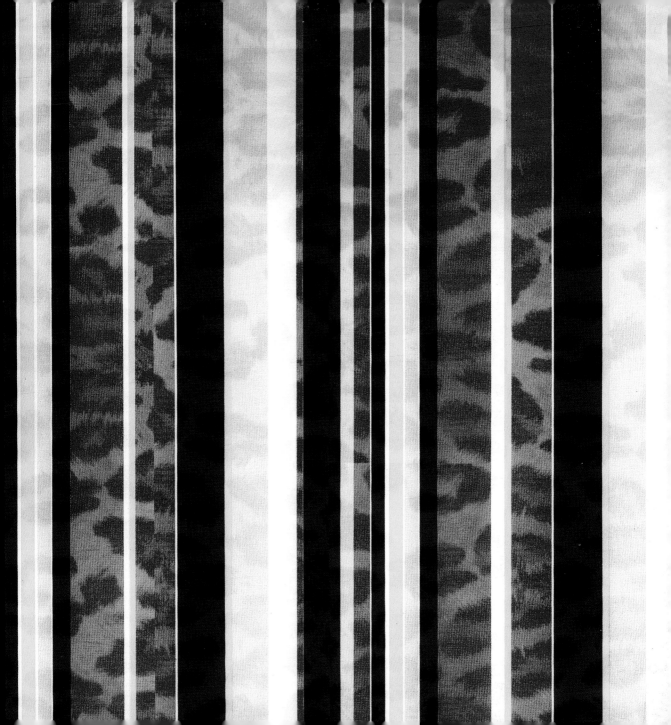

Names of Our Father

Yvonne Riley

MOODY
PUBLISHERS

All Scripture quotations, unless otherwise indicated, are taken from the Holy Bible, New Living Translation, copyright © 1996. Used by permission of Tyndale House Publishers, Inc., Wheaton, Illinois 60189, U.S.A. All rights reserved.

Scripture quotations marked NKJV are taken from the Holy Bible, New King James Version. Copyright © 1982 by Thomas Nelson, Inc. Used by permission. All rights reserved.

Scripture quotations marked The Message are taken from the Holy Bible, THE MESSAGE, Copyright © 1993, 1994, 1995, 1996, 2000, 2001, 2002. Used by permission of NavPress Publishing Group.

Scripture quotations marked NIV are taken from the Holy Bible, New International Version®. NIV®. Copyright © 1973, 1978, 1984 by International Bible Society. Used by permission of Zondervan Publishing House. All rights reserved.

Art Direction and Design: David Riley Associates, Newport Beach, CA. rileydra.com
Photography: Steve Anderson

ISBN: 0–8024–2946–7

1 3 5 7 9 10 8 6 4 2
Printed in Italy

THIS BOOK
belongs to:

A Special Word
to Parents and Adults

When the disciples of Jesus asked Him to teach them how to pray, He taught them a very special prayer. We call that prayer "The Lord's Prayer." We can learn from this simple model how to express our needs and our gratitude to God.

The Lord's Prayer offers to us hope, forgiveness and peace, but more importantly a bigger picture and deeper understanding of the One we call, "Our Father." We can learn more about God from what Jesus shares about His Father through this prayer. Jesus taught us to call God "Our Father" and we now have the honor to come to Him as His children.

In *Names of Our Father*, children can be taught about God and His divine character through His Hebrew names implied throughout the Lord's Prayer. Whether it is a child's first reading or a simple devotional you read with your child each day, I believe *Names of Our Father* will bring fresh insight to the greatest prayer ever recorded.

I have themed the book around different nations to illustrate the diversity of God's children. And once again, I have chosen a leopard to take us through the pages of this book.

I pray God will continue to open your eyes and the eyes of children everywhere more and more to the true meaning and privilege we have in calling God, "Our Father."

Yvonne Riley

"Behold what manner of love the Father has bestowed on us, that we should be called the children of God."

1 John 3:1

TABLE of CONTENTS

OuR PrAYeR

Our Dearest Father

Our Creator Who Lives and Rules from Heaven

Help Us to Live a Life that Honors Your Name

Remind Us that Our Real Home is in Heaven

Teach Us to Obey You

To do Your Will Here on Earth as it is Done in Heaven

Thank You, that Each Day You will Provide All We Need

Bless Us with Your Forgiveness as We Bless You by Forgiving Others

Lead Us Down the Right Path

Keep Us Safe and from Harm

For Your Splendor and Majesty are Always with Us

You are and will Always be The Great I Am!

ABBA

(ah~baa)

Everlasting

Loving

Merciful

Gracious

Good

Faithful

"But to all who believed him and accepted him,
he gave the right to become the children of God."

John 1:12

"Our Father..."

God wants to be our Father. He made us to know Him this way. That is why He sent His Son Jesus to the world—to show us the way back into His loving arms. Our sins kept us from God; there was a wall between God and us. But Jesus died on the cross in our place so we could be close to His Father in Heaven.

"Our Dearest Father..."

Abba means "Dearest Father." Long, long ago,
God decided to adopt us—to make us His children.
Just think, the Almighty God wants to
be our heavenly "Daddy." Thanks
to Jesus, we now have the
honor of becoming God's
beloved children and calling
Him Abba, Father.

ELOHIM
(e~lo~heem)

The Creator and Ruler of the Universe

The All-Powerful

The All-Knowing

The All-Wise

The Name given to The Trinity

"Before I formed you in the womb I knew you."
Jeremiah 1:5a (NKJV)

"Who Art in Heaven..."

At the very beginning of everything God created the heavens and the earth. That's the very first sentence in the Bible (Genesis 1:1)! In the beginning, **Elohim**, the Almighty Creator, gave His orders from Heaven and the whole world was made.

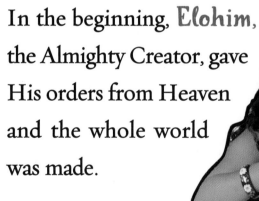

"Our Creator Who Lives and Rules from Heaven..."

Do you know how powerful God is? God our Father is so strong that His voice creates thunder. God our Father holds all the stars and planets in place. He tells the sun to rise each day and He tells the moon to shine bright at night. He is the most powerful in all the earth. God lives and reigns from Heaven. Every one of His children will also live in Heaven with Him forever!

KADDESH

(kad'~desh)

The Holy One

The One who Sanctifies

The One who Sets Apart

The One who Purifies

The Refiner

The Everlasting Light

"Long before God laid down earth's foundations,
he had us in mind, had settled on us as the focus of his love, to be made whole and
holy by his love."

Ephesians 1:4 *(The Message)*

"Hallowed be Thy Name..."

The name Kaddesh tells us that our God is Holy. That means that God can't do anything wrong or evil. He is perfect and pure in every way.

God wants us to be holy, too. Our Father wants us to live just as His Son, Jesus, did. This can make us sad as we realize we can't always do that. But there's good news! Kaddesh also means God our Father helps us to be like Jesus.

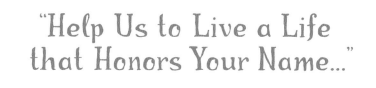

"Help Us to Live a Life that Honors Your Name..."

As we put our trust in God our Father, He gives us a new heart so we can become more like His Son. When His Spirit comes to live in us, He can make us to be more like Jesus, and this brings honor to His name!

NISSI

(nis~see)

He is My Banner

The Sign of Victory

The Symbol of His Power

The Promise of His Favor

The Pledge of His Presence

"May we shout for joy when we hear of your victory, flying banners to honor our God. May the Lord answer all your prayers."
Psalm 20:5

"Thy Kingdom come..."

Sometimes we have very bad days. Life on earth can often be hard to understand. The Bible tells stories of how God's people sometimes face difficult times. But when they followed God the Father, He always helped them to victory.

God's name **Nissi** describes Him as our banner or our cover. A banner is a symbol of God's presence and mighty power. This means He is always with us.

"Remind Us that Our Real Home is in Heaven..."

God's Kingdom is not here yet, but Jesus promised it would come soon. The name **Nissi** should always remind us that our forever home is in heaven. A perfect paradise with no more tears!

ADONAI

(a~do~ni')

Our Lord

Our Master and Owner

The One who Rules by Love

The One who Enables us to Obey Him

The One who Promises us His Presence

The One who Protects Us

"Remember that the Lord will give you an inheritance as your reward,
and the Master you are serving is Christ."
Colossians 3:24

"Thy Will be Done..."

For God's will to be done in our lives, we must learn to obey Him and follow His commands that are written in the Bible. God wants us to obey Him and to come to know Him as Adonai. That name means God our Father is also our Lord and Master and that we belong to Him. When we pray, "Thy will be done," we are letting God be in charge and we are asking Him to help us do things His way.

"Teach Us to Obey You..."

Sometimes following God's plan for our lives can be hard to do. But when we choose to obey God's will, He gives us the strength and the power to become obedient children who can call Him God, our Adonai!

SHALOM

(shal~lom')

The Source of Our Peace

He is Our Contentment

He is Our Fulfillment

He is Our Confidence

He is Our Rest

He is with Those Who are With Him

"The Lord gives his people strength. The Lord blesses them with peace."
Psalm 29:11

"On Earth as it is in Heaven..."

The name **Shalom** tells us that God our Father is our peace. Jesus made this possible for us to be at peace with God. When we live to obey Him, this peace will come to us as a result of our obedience to Him. There is nothing more fulfilling or satisfying

"To Do Your Will Here on Earth
as it is Done in Heaven..."

in life than to know we are pleasing our heavenly
Father and that He is smiling down on us.

EL sHADDAI

(el~sha'd~di)

The Giver of Gifts

The Source of all Blessings

The One who Nourishes

The One who Satisfies

The One who Supplies

The Almighty

"It is My Father who gives you the true bread out of heaven."
John 6:32 (NASB)

"Give Us this Day Our Daily Bread..."

El Shaddai means God our Father is the One who gives us all good gifts. He is the great "Giver of Life" and He lovingly provides for all our needs.

God created us to trust Him and when we go to Him for what we need it pleases Him. Each

"Thank You, that Each Day You will Provide All We Need..."

day we should begin by thanking God for always taking care of us and then we can ask Him to provide for what we need. It could be a prayer for our daily food or for even a right attitude. Only El Shaddai, the Almighty God, will always be there to answer our prayers.

ROPHE

(ro'~phay)

The One who Heals

The One who Restores

The Balm for Suffering

The Remedy for Our Sins

The Great Physician

The Tree of Life

"Have mercy on me, O God, because of your unfailing love.
Because of your great compassion, blot out the stain of my sins."
Psalm 51:1

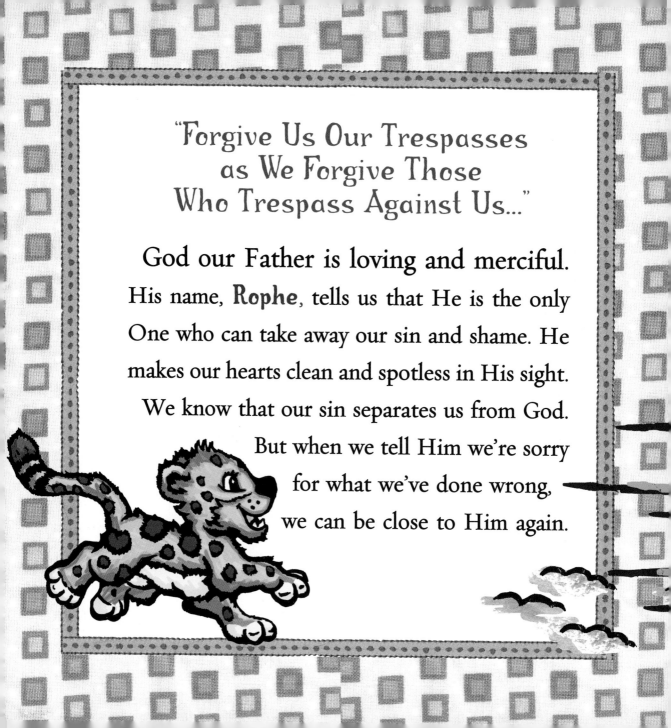

"Forgive Us Our Trespasses as We Forgive Those Who Trespass Against Us..."

God our Father is loving and merciful. His name, **Rophe**, tells us that He is the only One who can take away our sin and shame. He makes our hearts clean and spotless in His sight. We know that our sin separates us from God. But when we tell Him we're sorry for what we've done wrong, we can be close to Him again.

"Bless Us with Your Forgiveness as We Bless You by Forgiving Others..."

He not only forgives our sins, but forgets them. Our **Rophe** God wants to bless us by forgiving our sins and we can bless Him by forgiving each other!

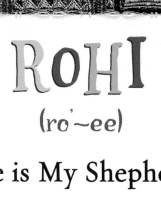

RoHI

(ro'~ee)

He is My Shepherd

He is My Companion

He is My Friend

He is My Protector

The One Who Leads

The One Who Feeds

*"He will feed his flock like a shepherd. He will carry the lambs in his arms,
holding them close to his heart."*

Isaiah 40:11

"Lead Us not Into Temptation..."

The name **Rohi** means God our Father is our Shepherd and we are His sheep. He will always keep us on the right path. When we put our trust in God, He shows us the road we should take and He shields us on every side.

"Lead Us Down the Right Path..."

If we are walking close to Him or following Him like sheep follow their Shepherd, we will be going the right way. God, our Rohi, will always watch over us and lead us down the right path.

JIREH

(yeer'~eh)

The Great Deliverer

The One Who Provides

The One Who Sees our Needs

The One Who Foresees

The One Who Reveals Himself
to His people

"The Lord protects his people and gives victory to his anointed king."
Psalm 28:8

"But Deliver Us from Evil..."

The name  Jireh means God our Father is the One who rescues us from danger. When God's children cry out to Him, He hears them and delivers them out of all their troubles. He is the Great Deliverer. He will save us when we are in danger.

The Bible calls the evil one Satan or the Devil. He is the one who would like

"Keep Us Safe and from Harm..."

to keep us from knowing how much God loves us. But let's remember that God is greater than he is. God watches over us and He protects us from harm. He is our hiding place and we don't have to be afraid because our Jireh God protects us.

SHAMMAH

(sham'~mah)

God is There

God's Presence Dwells
With His People

God Promises His Presence to be Felt

God Promises Rest

God Desires Us to Live
in His Kingdom Forever

"Who is the King of glory? The Lord Almighty—He is the King of glory."
Psalm 24:10

"For Thine is the Kingdom and the Power and the Glory..."

The name **Shammah** means that God our Father is always with us. God wants His presence to be real in our lives. Imagine the wonder of God's presence with us every day! God's kingdom is invisible but very, very real. His kingdom is in our hearts, and by His Holy Spirit living in us, we can feel His presence.

Jesus shows us what God's glory and power look like. When we read

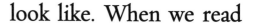

"For Your Splendor and Majesty are Always with Us..."

about Jesus in the Bible and see God's power and His incredible love, we see God—our **Shammah**. God shows the world His mighty power and glory through everything He made... and especially through His children!

JEHOVAH
(ja-ho'-vah)

The Name of the True God

Lord

The One who Always Was

The One who will Live Forever

The Unchangeable God

"I'm first, I'm last, and everything in between.
I'm the only God there is."
Isaiah 44:6 (The Message)

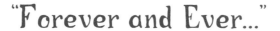

"Forever and Ever..."

All the names of God tell of His wonderful works and acts except one, Jehovah. The name Jehovah is the proper name for God that expresses who He is. It is also the name of the One True God, "The Great I Am."

As we choose to believe in Jehovah as the

"You are and will Always be The Great I Am!"

One and Only true God, we have the privilege of becoming His children. We will live forever and ever with our Jehovah, the One who always existed, the One who has no end, the One who will provide for our every need, and the One we call, "Our Father!"

Acknowledgements

I would like to gratefully acknowledge the team at Moody Publishers, especially Mark Tobey—for all the help with the editing of this book. Once again, it is an honor to be partnering with you all!

Thank You: Pamela and Jeannie for your continual support and encouragement. Lisa, Lindsay, Toni and Irene for all your hard work. My Tuesday Morning Prayer Group (Marilyn, Mae, Crystal, Cathe, Shelley, Kelly, Jeanne, and Jill), you are all such beautiful examples of godly women. Pastor Chuck Smith, you truly are "Papa Chuck" to so many of us. To my husband, David, you are my Ironman! And my darling ballerina daughter—Belle—you bring so much joy to my life and Mommy is very proud of you!!

Finally: James Hampton Riley—you have been a very loving father-in-law and the best "papa" to our family. We love you very much and I dedicate this book to you.

Raising Kids
in the FULLNESS OF GOD

Share with your children the joy of knowing God with two more books written by Yvonne Riley. *Jesus A to Z* and *Gift of the Spirit* are easy to read, beautifully illustrated books that give your child a complete picture of how God has revealed Himself to us.

Jesus A to Z $9.99
ISBN: 0-8024-2945-9

AVAILABLE NOW

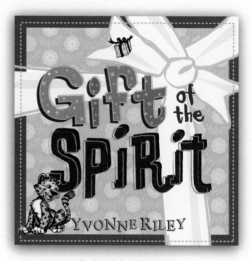

Gift of the Spirit $9.99
ISBN: 0-8024-2947-5

COMING SOON
TO A BOOKSTORE NEAR YOU!

DAVID and YVONNE RILEY, a husband and wife team, collaborated to create this series of children's books focused on the Trinity. Yvonne is a homemaker who writes out of her love for Jesus and children. David is the president of *David Riley Associates*, a graphic design/advertising agency in Newport Beach, California. They live with their daughter, Belle, and dog, Cosmo in Corona del Mar, California.